by Pip & Joy Wright

With thanks to the Suffolk Record Offices at
Ipswich, Bury St. Edmund's & Lowestoft,
and The Forum at Norwich.
Also to Mr. & Mrs. Mesquita for allowing us to photograph
objects found in the walls of their house

Rattlesden, where in 1645, two men and three women were *'found to be witches'* by Matthew Hopkins, the Witchfinder General

Published by **Pawprint Publishing**
14, Polstead Close, Stowmarket, Suffolk IP14 2PJ

ISBN 0 9548298 1 6

Cover design by William Alexander
Printed by Polstead Press, Stowmarket
First Reprint, June 2005
Second Reprint, April 2006
Third Reprint, April 2007
Forth Repint, December 2007
Fifth Reprint, July 2008
Sixth Reprint February 2009
Seventh Reprint, September 2009
Eighth Reprint, June 2010

Witches

in and around Suffolk

In April 1890, an inquest was held at Fressingfield in Suffolk on the body of a child who had died at the age of just eleven weeks. The parents were convinced that their daughter, **Edith Margaret Hammond**, had died due to the witchcraft of **Mrs. Corbyn**, the child's step-grandmother. The Daily News reported the case as follows: -

> *This woman died a few hours before the child, and stated that the child would not live long after her. The child was taken out in a perambulator, and the father stated that he saw smoke issue from the perambulator, and that the child died upon being taken home, the mother stating that it was hot and dry and smelt of brimstone. The medical evidence went to show that death was due to shock caused by the external application of some irritant, and the jury, in returning a verdict in accordance with the medical evidence said there was not sufficient evidence to show the nature of the irritant.* ***George Corbyn****, the child's grandfather said he was of opinion his late wife had the powers of a witch and he always tried to do what she wanted in consequence.*

For as long as history itself, we've been a superstitious lot in East Anglia. It is nearly 300 years since our elected representatives told us to stop persecuting witches, but old habits die hard. After all, if the Bible and Shakespeare recognised witches, who are we to disagree?

The trouble is, in a confusing world, it is comforting in a way to have an explanation for the inexplicable. Be it sickness or infestation, storm, blight or sudden death, then sorcery could just be the answer.

And magic can have its advantages... a little bit of advance warning of what the future is about to throw at you could be worth its weight in a palm crossed with silver. Spells and concoctions could be designed to make you more attractive, more successful, more fertile; or just incapacitate the opposition, leaving your way open to the success you seek.

A whole folk-lore has grown up around the 'wise ones' of Suffolk, so that in most of our towns and villages, you can still find someone who will tell you tales of their local *'witch'*.

The Kettlebaston village web-site contains a faded photograph of **Mumphsy Brett** taken outside the stone cottage where she lived less than a century ago. Tradition has it that her powers of witchcraft were never more obvious than when her husband and son defied her wishes by setting off for Bildeston without her. In her anger, she worked a spell that left the pair of them unable to move from their donkey-cart for the rest of the day.

But truth to tell, the history of witchcraft in and around Suffolk is an altogether darker story, about suffering, persecution and death. It reached into the hearts of families and communities and created a fear and a hysteria that lasted until recent times.

Early cases of witchcraft in Eastern England

Throughout the Middle-Ages, both Christianity and folk-witchcraft existed side by side without giving rise to the inquisitions that plagued Europe. White witches, working as herbalists and midwives enjoyed the air of mysticism that surrounded them, and even kings took their advice.

Also, in the eyes of the public, such people were no better, no worse, than many of their clergy. Though priests were meant to observe a vow of chastity, clearly, many did not. Extraordinary numbers of them found themselves indicted at the Assizes in the early 15th century for rape and for being *'common ravishers of women'*. In 1401, **John Davy**, vicar of Brent Eleigh; **John Cosyn**, parson of Gedding; **Stephen Ganen**, the chaplain of Fornham St. Genevieve; Nicholas, chaplain of Culford and **John**, parson of Aldham were all summoned to answer this charge. In 1405, four more Suffolk priests met the same fate, including **Stephen Nycole** of Hepworth, who was accused of raping three servants.

If the priests were bad, what about the witches?

Accurate evidence, especially regarding early witchcraft cases, is very hard to obtain. Take for example **Margery Jourdemaine** of Eye, supposed by some writers to have been consulted by Henry VI when Parliament met at Bury St. Edmunds in 1447. She had 'advised' a number of eminent men and women of her day including Eleanor Cobham, wife of the Duke of Gloucester, who was banished for conspiring to take the life of the king by magic. It is possible that the king felt it was safer to have Margery Jourdemaine on his side rather than against him. However, the truth appears to have been rather different. A known diviner, *'The Witch of Eye'* was first arrested with two priests in 1432 for sorcery, but released. According to several sources she was tried in 1441 with Thomas Southwell and Roger Bolingbroke, accused of using sorcery in seeking to know the date of the death of Henry VI.

She was burned for treason, whilst her more noble accomplices were hanged, drawn and quartered.

Though witches suffered far more in Scotland, they were largely tolerated here, but after all, much of the supernatural activity that was their stock in trade was similar to those practices employed by the Roman Catholic Church at the time. An article published in the Suffolk Chronicle, October 20th 1810 described such a ceremony.

EXTRAORDINARY CUSTOM
FORMERLY PRACTISED BY THE MONKS
OF BURY ST. EDMUND'S, SUFFOLK

The religious fathers of this monastery had propagated an opinion, that if any married woman that had no children, and wished to become a mother, would but come with a white bull to the shrine of St. Edmund, and make her offerings and vows, she should presently after obtain her desire; and as it was usual to institute processions, to give great dignity and solemnity to the ceremony, it was thought necessary to have a very public one on this important occasion, and for this purpose, a white bull was provided, elegantly adorned with garlands of flowers, ribbons, &c. which being led by one of the monks, the petitioning lady at the same time following him, and often stroking his milk-white side, the procession thus proceeded through Churchgate and Guildhall streets, and along the Cook-Row down to the great West-gate of the abbey, attended by the monks singing, accompanied with a prodigious concourse of people, forming a very numerous cavalcade. - The bull being dismissed, the lady entered the church, advanced to St. Edmund's shrine, said her prayers, made her offering at his altar, kissing the stone, and entreating with tears, the blessing of a child, she then returned from the abbey with full assurance of speedy success. This custom had gained so much credit in many parts of the world, that not only many eminent women of this country had recourse to it, but even several ladies belonging to foreign parts. But as it would be very inconvenient for those distant ladies to come in person to perform these ceremonies, it was pronounced to be equally efficacious for them, if they caused to be offered by any other means, one of these wonder working animals at St. Edmund's shrine. A copy of a deed was formerly, and probably at the present time is preserved in the Augmentation Office, to the following effect; "That John Swaffham, sacrist of the monastery of St. Edmund's Bury, certifies to all Christian people, that on the 2nd June 1474, three religious persons, (whom he names) of the city of Ghent, came and offered, as has been accustomed of old time, in the presence of several reputable people, at the shrine of the blessed king, virgin, and martyr, St. Edmund, to the honour of God, and of the said glorious martyr, one white bull, for the accomplishment of the longing of a certain noble lady."

Of course, your local friendly witch would have done it all a lot cheaper. But whilst the church may not have cornered the market in superstitious rites, they could be relied on to offer some good ones. The following story comes from Froude's *'Short studies on great subjects'*.

A Suffolk yeoman, **William of Ramsholt**, had invited a party to a feast. A neighbour had made him a present of a cheese and his little daughter Beatrice had been directed to put it away in a safe place. Beatrice did as she was told, but went to play with her brother, Hugh, and forgot what she had done with it. The days went on, the feast was near. The children hunted in every corner of the house, but no cheese could be found. The nearest town was far off. They had no money to buy another if they could reach it, and a whipping became sadly probable. An idea struck little Hugh. "Sister," he said, "I have heard that the blessed Thomas (à Becket) is good and kind. Let us pray to Thomas to help us." They went to their beds, and, as Hugh foretold, the saint came to them in their dreams. "Don't you remember," he said, "the old crock in the back kitchen, where the butter used to be kept?" They sprang up and all was well.

Finding lost objects was just one of a number of services offered by the church, but also by local *'naughty people'* and their *'imps.'* These are the stuff of folk-tales and legends. Several old stories come down to us today by way of the pen of **Ralph de Coggeshall**, a medieval monk with a fascination for the bizarre. In one such tale, a grotesque imp called Malekin was sent to haunt a house at Dagworth before it was captured and imprisoned for seven years (Another version describes this house as a castle, in which case, it must refer to nearby Haughley). One tale from the days of Henry II describes how an evil spirit entered the body of a drowned man at Orford and haunted those shores until caught by fishermen. His body was covered with hair and his beard reached his waist. When he was taken to church he never crossed himself or bent his knee before the altar. He only awoke during the hours of darkness and finally escaped back to the open sea.

Witchcraft in Tudor Times

Whilst magic was merely a cause for wonder it appears to have been accepted in this part of the world. However, during Tudor times Kings, Queens, and those close to them became ever fearful of any force that might be used against them. The unpopularity of Anne Boleyn came about in part from the belief that she had bewitched King Henry VIII. She was reputed to have six fingers on one hand and even a third teat, believed to be signs of a witch.

Witchcraft in itself had never been a crime, though causing death by magic clearly had. After Henry VIII's reformation, heresy and superstition became big issues, reaching the point of public paranoia. The following tales come from a book published in 1562 by **Dr. William Bullein**, entitled *'Defence against all sickness, sornes, and woundes that dooe daily assaulte mankinde'*. Dr. Bullein was rector of Blaxhall in Suffolk before turning his talents to medicine and making his name as a surgeon in London.

> *I dyd know wythin these few years a false Witch called* ***M(other) Line****, in a town of Suffolk called Parham, which with a payre of Ebene beades and certain charmes, had no small resort of foolysh women when their chyldren were syck. To thys lame Witch they resorted to have the Fairie charmed and the Spyute*

coniured away: through the prayers and the Ebene beades whych she sayd came from the holy land and were santifyed at Rome. Through whom many goodly cures have been don, but my chaunce was to burn ye sayd beads. Oh! That damable witches be suffered to lieu unpunished and so many blessed men burned: witches be more hurtful in this realm than either quarten, pox, or pestilence. I knew in a towne called Kelshall in Suffolk a Witch whose name was ***M(other) Didge,*** *who with certain Aue Maries upon her Ebene Beades and a waxe Candle, used this Charme folowyng for S. Anthonies fyre, having the sicke body before her, holding up her Hande saying: there came two Angels out of the North east, one brought fyre the other brought frost, out fyre and in frost. In nomine patris, etc. I could reherse an C of sutch knackes of these holy gossips, the fyre take them all, for they be God's enemyes.*

Though there were attempts to draft anti-witchcraft laws, it took until 1563 for the Witchcraft Act to appear on the statute books.

Almost immediately three women in Chelmsford were accused, tried and received dramatically different sentences.

Elizabeth Francis was said to have conspired with her familiar, a black cat called Sathan to seduce young men, one of whom she married. According to her confession, Sathan was responsible for the death of her child and the laming of her husband with whom she had *'become dissatisfied'*. She received one year's imprisonment, but hanged three years later after facing trial for witchcraft again.

Agnes, known as **Mother Waterhouse** admitted to purchasing the cat Sathan, with whose help she had killed a number of animals belonging to people she did not like. She also admitted to the killing of one William Fynee. She was found guilty and hanged two days later.

Joan Waterhouse, her daughter, was accused by somewhat unconvincing witnesses of training a black dog to open doors with a magic key and stab people with a knife held in its mouth. The court did not believe the accusations and she was released.

The 1563 act did not link witchcraft with the devil or with religious heresy, and only condemned to death those who committed murder. Though the rest of Europe burned witches, this act prescribed death by hanging for… *"who shall use practise or exercise any witchcrafte enchantment charme or sorcerie whereby any person shall happen to be killed or destroyed"*. Lesser witchcraft offences were punishable by up to a year's imprisonment and a spell in the pillory.

A copy of a document at Bury Record Office dating back to the 1580s, lists punishments to be administered to offenders in St. Mary's parish in Bury, whereby anyone... *"proved to be a witche, inchaunter or sowthesayer is to be punished according to the law."* Those merely accused publicly were to be imprisoned until sureties were lodged with the magistrates to ensure their good behaviour. In this document, witchcraft appears to be classed with such misdemeanours as blasphemy, fornication, drunkenness & absence from church on a Sunday.

In 1582 at St. Osyth (written St. Oses in old documents) in Essex, what started as a series of village quarrels led to 13 women being tried for witchcraft and belonging to a witches' coven. This trial, the details of which were published at the time, introduced a number of the features that were to become common at witch trials over the next hundred years or more.

Nearly 350 years later, these events would lead to a remarkable discovery.

Elizabeth Bennet had a number of *'familiars'* including a spirit *'looking much like a ferret'* (could it possibly have been a ferret?), a black dog and a hare which she sent to kill William Byett's cattle, but instead it killed his wife. Though she was promised clemency if she confessed, she was convicted and hanged.

Ursley (Ursula) Kempe confessed she had sent her grey cat, Tittey to bring sickness upon John Thorlowe's wife. Her eight-year old son described how spirits came in the night time, to *"sucke blood of her upon her armes and other places of her body"*. Of the accused, she was the only other one to hang, though four women were found guilty but reprieved. These were **Ales (Alice) Newman**, **Ales Glascocke**, **Cysley (Cecily) Celles** and **Joan Turner**. A feature of this trial was the way in which the women were persuaded to testify against one another, almost clambering over each another to get into the witness box and relate another even more fantastic story.

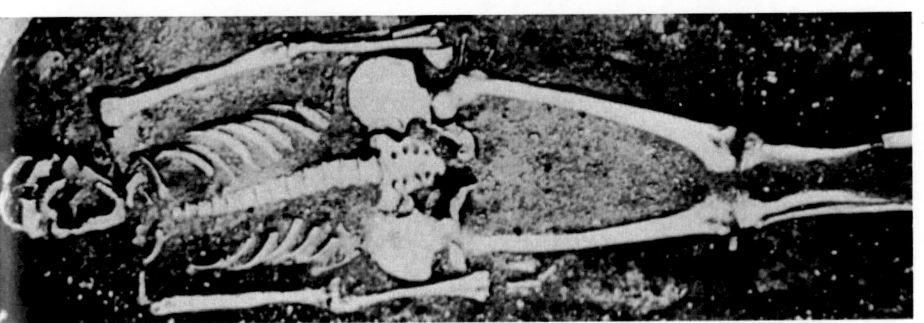

This skeleton was dug up in a garden in St. Osyth in 1921. It is believed to be the remains of one of two women hanged for witchcraft in 1582. It did not go without mention in newspaper reports of the time that her face looked as if had been screaming for over 300 years.

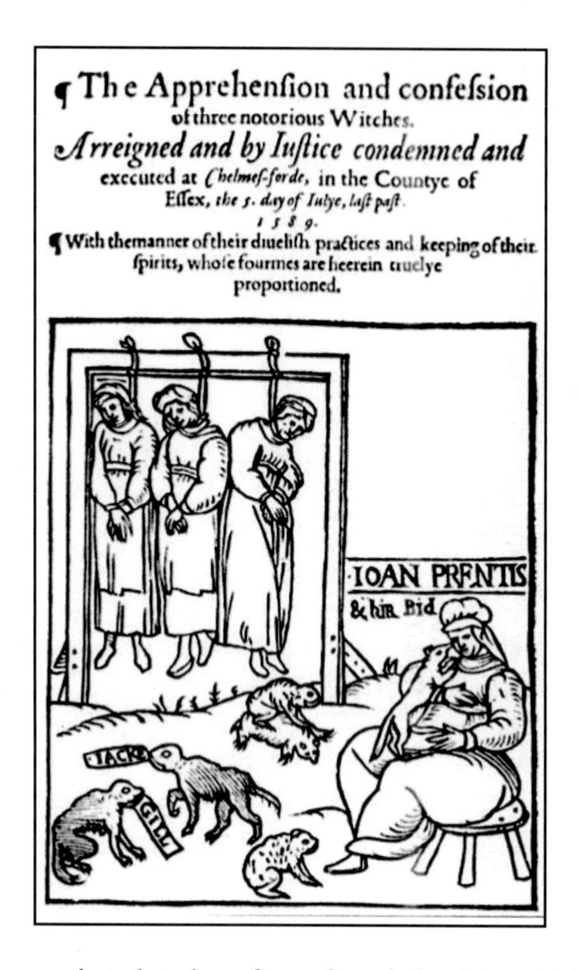
¶ The Apprehension and confession of three notorious Witches.
Arreigned and by Iustice condemned and executed at *Chelmes-forde*, in the Countye of Essex, *the 5. day of Iulye, last past.* 1589.
¶ With the manner of their diuelish practices and keeping of their spirits, whose fourmes are heerein truelye proportioned.

Essex continued to be a focus for witch trials, which sometimes led to rapid justice. At the trial of the three Joans in 1589, a Chelmsford judge condemned **Joan Upney**, **Joan Cony** and **Joan Prentice** to death. They were hanged within two hours of leaving the court, and details of their trial sold.

Across the country in a number of prosecutions, children testified against their parents and grandparents. At Pendle in Lancashire, **Jennet Device**, aged nine, gave evidence that led to the deaths of her mother and her sister.

The parish register of Wells, in Norfolk describes how the deaths of 13 men at sea in 1583 were *"brought to pas by the detestable working of an execrable witch of Kings Lynn whose name was* ***Mother Gabley****: by the boyling, or rather labouring of certeyne eggs in a payle full of cold water, afterward proved sufficiently at the arraignment of ye said witch."*

Oliffe or **Doll Barthram** of Stradbroke was accused of sending three toads to destroy the rest of Joan Jordan, which set fire to her house. Others in the parish, including the constable and the vicar testified in her trial at Bury that she had sent a spirit in the form of a cat called Gyles down the chimney of Joan Jordan to kill her. Also, it was said that she had killed an unborn child by *'nipping out his brains'*. She hanged at Bury on July 12th 1599.

Some 'witches' really did bring about the deaths of their neighbours. With a scattering of folk-herbalists and self-styled alchemists possessing an active knowledge of how to produce poisons and narcotics, evidently, mistakes were bound to be made. Such people were a focus of gossip and rumour; and, above all, dread. With digitalis, they could induce sleep; with ergot, came hallucination. Ancient poisons such as aconite, wolfbane, belladonna and hemlock were so toxic that only minute concentrations could cause delirium and death. People with the knowledge of their preparation and effects were to be feared if not respected.

To bring witches to trial required the collecting of spurious 'evidence' and the preparing of a case. This was sometimes the province of the witch hunters. One such character was **John Parkhurst** of Norfolk. Exiled during the reign of Mary, he spent time in Europe experiencing the anti-witch blood-lust that had gripped the continent. He returned, determined to use this experience to rid Norfolk of witches. It is known he indicted at least fourteen witches, leading to the execution of five.

The most infamous of these was **Margaret Read**, who was burned as a witch in Kings Lynn in 1590. You can still see the mark on the wall where her black spirit is supposed to have leapt from her body to escape the flames.

The Seventeenth Century

When James I took the throne of England, he came with a long-felt fear of witches and had already published a book about the finding of witches. Under James, the law took on a new intensity. To hang, you no longer had to be guilty of murder by way of sorcery. Just being a witch was a capital offence. Towards the end of his life, there is plenty of indication that King James altered his way of thinking, and would have repealed his 1603 Act if it had been politically possible to do so. But the damage had been done. Anti-witch fervour had taken over. As the seventeenth century unravelled, more and more people sought reasons for every unfortunate event in their lives. What had once been regarded as 'God's will' now caused people to cry 'Witchcraft!' When misfortune came about, any old lady living nearby (90% of all the witches ever tried were women; most of them elderly) who mumbled to herself, behaved oddly or kept pets was a likely suspect. In his book *'A guide to Grand Jurymen with respect to Witches'* (1627), Richard Bernard explained why the devil was so keen on recruiting women.

1. Satan is setting on these rather than on men, since his unhappy onset and prevailing with Eve.
2. Their more credulous nature, apt to be misled and deceived.
3. For they are commonly impatient, and more superstitious… more malicious… and far more revengeful and so herein more fit instruments of the Devil.
4. They are more tongue ripe, and less able to hide what they know from others, & therefore… more ready to be teachers of witchcraft to others.
5. And lastly, because they think they can command, they are more proud in their rule, and more busy in setting on such work whom they may command, than men.

Witches could be identified, it was believed, by their closeness to animals, which became their *'familiars.'* Some were reputed to be able to change shape and become *'as cats and hares.'* Witches, it was said, robbed graves for bodies as part of their fiendish spells. The bodies of children were specially potent. Witches were reputed to have the power to cause a corpse to bleed. Generally, though, anyone that had unusual bodily marks or was given to lewdness and cursing could be regarded as a witch.

Having identified your witch, what was needed was a reliable means of proving her guilt.

In order to bring a witch to trial, there must be witnesses, however young, unreliable or implausible; and the more the better.

It was useful to be able to show that a witch had been marked by the devil as belonging to him. Such marks were said to be places on the body where the witch could not feel pain. Prickers were employed, using a variety of knives and probes to test their victims for *'devil's marks'.* This was very open to abuse. There is evidence that retractable pointers were used. Also applying a tourniquet would numb a limb enough for the pricker to achieve the desired result.

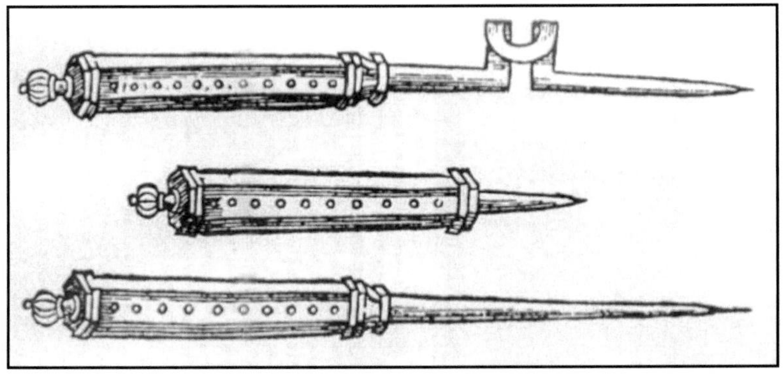

The pricker's tools

It was said that all witches possessed a third nipple, sometimes more, in order to suckle the Devil or his disciples. These could be searched for in the most intimate parts of a witch's body and all manner of warts and imperfections would be accepted as the devil's teats. It is worth remembering that modern medical research shows that 7% of women and 9% of men have an extra teat anyway.

Probably the most famous test of whether someone was a witch was to swim her. Ordeal by water had been popular in Saxon times; now it was adapted to fit the trial of suspected witches. She was tied crossways - the right thumb to the left big toe, and the left thumb to the right big toe. She was ducked as prayers were spoken; if she sank she was considered innocent, but if she floated she was guilty. Having rejected the holy water of her baptism, it was assumed the water would in turn reject a witch. According to the witchcraft laws then in operation the result of such a swimming was not acceptable as evidence, though it formed an important part of the evidence offered in many 17th century trials. It was not intended that the innocent should drown, though there were cases of recipients of this procedure who never recovered. Nevertheless, people had such faith in it that many accused women asked to be swum as a way of proving their innocence.

Of course there was nothing like a confession to secure a conviction, though how these confessions were obtained was a cause for concern, even then. As will shortly be shown, **Matthew Hopkins**, the Witchfinder General could guarantee to 'persuade' almost any accused witch to confess. Such confessions could be bizarre in the extreme.

One final test rarely accepted in court, but popular with a gullible peasantry, was weighing the witch against the big Bible in the parish church. Many believed that witches flew because they were unnaturally light. If the Bible was heavier than they were, it proved their guilt.

The Cunning People

As ever more witches were brought for trial, the public looked for protection against such evil. In some cases they turned to the church; at other times to *'cunning people'* with the power to offer protective remedies. Some of these became legends in their own right, such as **Cunning Herring**, "*a cawker of Sudbery*,"(1582) who could find witches and protect people against their spells. "**Old Creek** of Cobduck" (Copdock) (1591) could help bring good fortune your way. **Gilbert Wakering**, a surgeon from Halstead (1620) could help find lost goods. **Mother Hoveye** of Hadleigh (1645) was active in the seeking out of witches.

In addition to a vast array of cures, preserving charms and spell breakers, the cunning people risked being accused themselves of the very witchcraft they claimed to be able to counteract. **Joseph Glanvil**, in his 1689 book '*A full and plain evidence concerning Witches and Apparitions*', told a story of a fellow from Cambridge who boarded in a house in Suffolk where the landlord's wife had long been haunted by a thing in the shape of a bird that would *'flurr near her face'* so she could never rest. An old man who made her acquaintance said it was a dead sprite that had to be treated using a witch bottle.

He advised him to take a bottle and put some of the woman's urine into it together with hair, pins, nails and needles, then cork it and put it into the fire. Eventually, the bottle blew its cork and its contents flew about the room, but the curse continued. (Only if the bottle exploded in the fire would it kill the witch) The old man then bade her bury a similar bottle to that she had placed in the fire. This done, the wife began to find things better. But a woman living some distance away announced that her husband had been killed by this piece of magic. He was a wizard, who had bewitched the landlord's wife, and he had suffered from the counter-charm.

Bellarmine 'witch' bottles

There are many tales told about witch bottles. Bellarmine bottles, with their distinctive bearded faces on, were believed to have been designed for such a purpose.

In a pair of articles that appear in Volumes 28 and 30 of the proceedings of Suffolk Institute of Archaeology, Norman Smedley described the finding of a number of Bellarmine bottles in Suffolk that appeared to have been used as *'Witch bottles'*. Some, like a number found in the 1950s had grotesque faces on: others like one uncovered during the excavations for the foundations for the new Ipswich (Civic) College in 1958 were similar, but lacked the mask, having instead horseshoe designs on the outside. Scientific examination of a number of those discovered in Suffolk show the typical contents to have been iron nails, pins, pointed sticks, human hair, nail clippings and phosphates (denoting the presence once of urine).

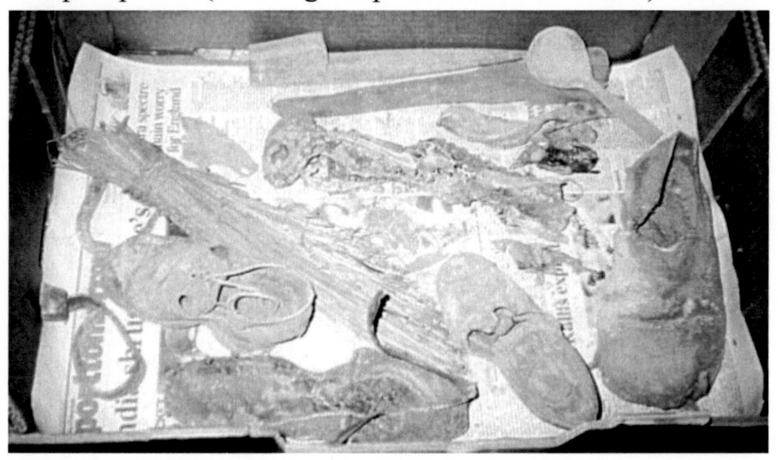

Modern house renovations often yield good luck charms in walls & chimneys such as mummified cats, silver coins, shoes and horse-skulls (even witches' brooms). This picture of such a cache found recently in Old Newton is typical. Local historian, Tim Easton, refers to such a collection as a *spiritual midden*. These objects were there to keep the evil spirits out, and even in more sceptical times today, it is interesting to note how many are put back. After all, you never know!

There were many ways of limiting a witch's power. Making her bleed, breaking her cartwheels, snapping her broomstick or merely using the traditional charms such as horseshoes above doorways were reputed to give you a fair measure of protection. According to **John Glyde**, the 19th century historian, Stanningfield Church had a glazed tile beside the threshold of the South door, in the shape of a horseshoe, for this very purpose. A panel on the font in Woodbridge Church shows an imp being ejected through the door of the church porch. A low stall in Thrandeston Church boasts carvings of two very 'witchy' figures. One woman is hitching up her skirt in a most un-churchlike way. She and another hag are clutching their 'familiars' - a cat and an owl.

Well into the nineteenth century, people were seeking advice and protection from the 'wise ones' of their community. In Ipswich in the 1820s, a white wizard known as '**Old Winter**' plied his trade. **James Murrell** of Hadleigh in Essex, who died around 1860, lived in a remote tarred shack beside the river. People still concerned about witches in their midst would beat a path to his door, prepared to pay the standard rate of one penny for his herbal remedies. Some came to be freed from spells and curses. Many said he was a wizard, though he was known far and wide as '**Cunning Murrell**', and together with his son, Buck, and his daughter, Alice, he could find lost animals, create love-potions; even, it was said, see through walls. An article about his witch-bottle activities can be read in 'Newspapers in Suffolk: Vol. 5' by Pip & Joy Wright. It was reported that when James Murrell died, sacks of letters were found in his hut from people requesting his help.

The Witchfinder General

The 17th century was a time of social and religious change. It was also a time of civil war, with all the confusion that was bound to bring. Which brings us to that infamous character **Matthew Hopkins**, the self-styled '**Witchfinder General**'

who travelled East Anglia, briefly earning a comfortable living, finding and bringing to trial hundreds of witches across six counties. Moving across the Puritan Parliament-supporting heartland, he forced confessions from those he had been paid to find and bring to trial. In August 1645, two hundred witches were tried at Bury St. Edmunds: 124 presented to the court by Matthew Hopkins. It has been suggested in a number of books that 68 of these were hanged, though this is probably a bit of an exaggeration.

Matthew Hopkins, pictured here, is reputed to have been the son of John (or James) Hopkins, vicar of Wenham in Suffolk. He almost certainly practised law in Manningtree and Ipswich, so… "*it follows that he was skilled in presenting a convincing case without the necessity of believing in its authenticity.*" (Witchcraft in British History - Ronald Holmes)

The law of England forbade torture as a means of extracting a confession, but Hopkins pushed the definition of torture to its limit. Take his first case for example. He first denounced a poor one-legged hag named **Elizabeth Clarke** of Manningtree as a witch, suggesting she led a coven and offered up sacrifices to the devil.

Upon examination, the damning third teat was found on her body, but it took three days and nights constant 'walking' to exhaust her to the extent she was prepared to confess to having five imps in the form of dogs and cats, which she suckled from her extra teats (which were almost certainly warts). In her confession, she implicated five other women, suggesting they were her 'accomplices'. They in their turn gave the names of others. Of those arrested, four died in prison before their trial, and as many as nineteen may have hanged.

Their confessions, though improbable-sounding to us today, became the standard fare of witch trials for the next year or so. Imps and familiars were reputed to have been given names such as 'Pyewacket, Elemanzer and Grizzel Greedigut', names which Hopkins said, *"no mortal could invent."*

The success of this trial, and subsequent ones in the Manningtree area, led Hopkins and his team of assistants to move into Suffolk where they were offered payments for the finding of witches in communities where hysteria had started to take root. In addition to Hopkins himself, there was **John Sterne**, his second-in-command, **Goody Phillips**, (an expert searcher for 'witch marks'), **Edward Parsley** and **Frances Mills**.

In these times of Puritanism, the explicit sexual content shocked and excited the population of Suffolk.

Mary Bush, a widow from Bacton, (sometimes incorrectly listed as Barton) said in her testimony that the devil came to her as a young black man, who asked her for blood which he drew out of her mouth and dropped on a sheet of paper which he wrapped up and carried away. She said he was *'colder than man and heavier, and could not performe nature as man.'* **Rebecca West** and **Ellen Greenleife**, both of the same village confessed to praying to the devil, referring to him as *'my God.'*

The image of the devil in human form was repeated in many of the confessions. **Elizabeth Richmond** of Bramford confessed the devil appeared to her in the likeness of a man called Daniel the Prophet. **Thomazine Ratcliffe** of Shelley said he appeared to her as a man with cloven hooves who spoke with a hollow shrill voice.

Elizabeth Southerne of Dunwich claimed that another witch, **Mother Collit** had sent the devil to her in the form of a crab. Climbing into her bed he had nipped her and drunk her blood, so sealing a covenant and promising to provide for her. After that she claimed he lay with her a number of times in different forms, once as a hairy black boy, just ten years old.

Margaret Bennet of Bacton said in her confession that … *"the devil in the shape of a man... carried her body over a close into a thicket of bushes and there lay with her, and after scratched her hand with the bushes and took her hand into his hand and writ upon a black patch, but she knew not what."*

Goody Smith of Bramford was supposed to have kept her imps hanging in a bag, hidden in her secret parts.

The *'Devil's List'* Hopkins claimed he had was growing ever longer. The witch trials of 1645 are well documented. Parish and Borough accounts show the expense of bringing witches to trial. At Aldeburgh, the following payments appeared in the records for that year.

	£	s	d
To Goody Phillips for her pains in searching out witches	1	0	0
To Widow Phillips, the search woman, for giving evidence	1	5	0
To John Paine for hanging seven witches	0	11	0
To William Dannell for the gallows and setting them up	1	0	0
For a post to set by the grave of the dead bodies that were hanged and for burying of them	0	6	0
Received of Mr. Newgate in part for trying a witch	4	0	0
Received of Mr. Richard Browne by the hands of Bailiff Johnson in part for trying a witch	4	0	0
To Mr. Hopkyns in the town for finding out witches	2	0	0

For all that, Aldeburgh were hedging their bets, as the same book shows that the town paid 5s. *"...to one Richards, a poor man, to go to the woman of Stowmarket for the remedy of his disease."* After all, there was little difference between a witch and what the country folk regarded as a 'blesser'.

Though Hopkins claimed 20 shillings would suffice to cover his expenses when invited to visit a town or village, where records exist, they show he received rather more. The Aldeburgh accounts show that Hopkins and his team received a total of £6. Stowmarket records show that Hopkins was paid £28 in all for the finding of seven witches, whilst at Kings Lynn he and his deputy, John Sterne were paid £15. Most places got their money's worth.

Other parishes in Suffolk where the number of witches tried totalled four or more were Framlingham (10), Halesworth (7), Bramford (6), Ipswich (6), Rattlesden (5), Wickham (5), Bacton (4), Copdock (4), Hintlesham (4), Chattisham (5) and Glemham (9).

The testimonies of the accused and the prosecution witnesses survive intact in many cases. These often bear a marked similarity to one another, suggesting words were put into people's mouths in order to achieve the desired effect - a conviction. Unfortunately, what is often unclear is what the final outcome was. One hundred and seventeen names are listed in Richard Deacon's book *'Matthew Hopkins - Witchfinder General'*, but this cannot be the complete Suffolk list as it names no-one from Hoxne or Aldeburgh where evidence remains that Hopkins was paid to find witches. We can only be sure of the execution of 21 of Deacon's list of 117, with another six who probably hanged. The commonly quoted figure is 68, though its accuracy is doubtful. A likely source of this estimated figure of deaths from the Hopkins trials is a book entitled *'An Historical Essay Concerning Witchcraft'* written by Dr. F. Hutchinson in the early 18th century. It should be remembered that although this book was written little more than half a century after the event, his estimates are only estimates, however often they may have been quoted since.

A handful of people accused of witchcraft are known to have been acquitted: as regards the rest, some reappear in their parish records at a latter date. Here are two such cases from the trials of 1645.

Ellen wife of **Nicholas Greenleife** of Bacton confessed she had welcomed the devil into her bed, but only out of fear because he had threatened to tear her in pieces, *"wch did much affright her."* She said she had caused Hogard's mare to become lame and sent lice to Mr. Lockwood. She seems to have returned to her parish and been buried there (in consecrated ground) in August 1656.

Mary Scrutton of Framlingham told the court she was plagued by imps that *"kept a sqeakeinge."* She said the devil appeared to her in the guise of a bear and tempted her in a hollow voice to kill her child. Then, he met her *"like a man and took her by the arme,"* but what he told her she would not say. Her funeral appears in the Framlingham burial register 23 years later.

For the most part, those arraigned in court had confessed. The exception to the rule was at Glemham where a conspiracy of silence seems to have been successful in creating difficulties in constructing prosecution cases. **Ann** and **Mary Smith**, however, did, after two days and nights without sleep confess to employing their imps in the destruction of cattle belonging to their neighbours and selling their imps to **Bet Bray** of Stradbroke. Also they sold one to lame **Goody Barker** so it would *"get betwixt her husband and herself."* The Smith girls' openness seems to have done them little good as both probably hanged. Bet Bray was arrested soon after. It is not known what happened to her.

Seventeen of the 117 listed were men. Four of them are known to have hanged. Just three married couples were tried. **James** and **Mary Emmerson** of Ipswich were acquitted of murder and witchcraft. **Thomas** and **Mary Everard** of Halesworth were less fortunate.

When given 'the treatment' by Hopkins and his team, Thos. Everard was the first to break. He confessed to loving the devil and denying God, saying an imp, appearing like a rabbit took blood from behind his ear and suckled from his teats. After that, he sent his imps to kill *"a deere and a rotten sheepe"* before arranging the killing of Irish John Woods, his children and his own grandchild and his wife. Thomas and Mary Everard, along with at least three of the other five Halesworth witches were hanged. Their daughter, **Mariana**, was given the benefit of the doubt and was reprieved.

Mary and **Nathaniel Bacon** of Chattisham confessed to the usual collection of imps, compacts with the devil, and finally to the murder of their own children. Mary Bacon said she had sent her imp to kill her daughter and she wished her son's child *"cold in the mouth"* and it died likewise. A feature of the Chattisham witches and those from nearby Copdock was their willingness to involve one another in their testimonies, so at least six of them, including Mary Bacon were hanged. Nathaniel's fate is not known.

The frontispiece from Hopkins' book

The ways by which Matthew Hopkins and his colleagues secured confessions are well known. Hopkins made his methods crystal clear when, seeking to justify himself to his critics, he published *"The discovery of witches"* in 1647. By this time many were doubtful of his sincerity and his conduct. Hopkins replied to a series of questions about the means he employed to extract confessions, denying the use of violence and torture.

However, he confirmed his belief in 'watching' (sleep deprivation), 'walking' and 'swimming'. He claimed he had no part in 'flattery' (promising to go easy on someone who is prepared to confess). He denied believing in or using as evidence the improbable, such as flying on broomsticks. He denied putting words into people's mouths - *"You have four imps, haven't you, and they come to you in the shape of toads, don't they?"*

But Hopkins' credibility was short lived. One or two high profile cases left a bad taste in the mouth and a mountain of resentment was left behind him as he moved on into Norfolk and Cambridgeshire. One such case was that of the Reverend **John Lowes**, vicar of Brandeston, which showed that the more unpopular you were, the more likely you were to find witnesses prepared to offer all manner of testimony against you. This case is dealt with in detail in *'Witch hunting and Witch trials'* by C. L'Estrange Ewen.

Forty-eight years as vicar at Brandeston had not made 80 year-old **John Lowes** a popular man. He was an uninspiring preacher. He was a Royalist at a time when Cromwell's supporters held sway. He had regularly taken his neighbours to court over petty matters and when an investigation was started, several came forward to testify against him. Reports from the time state that the old man was kept awake for several nights, after which Hopkins' men ran him up and down the room till exhausted and caring little for life, he confessed to sending his imps to sink ships between Yarmouth and Winterton and causing *'the child of Nathaniel Mann to languish and die.'* He was also swum, though reports suggest he fared no better or worse than others that day. Though he tried to retract his statement at his trial, he was still found guilty and condemned to hang. Denied a priest to read a funeral service for him, he is said to have recited it as he went to the gallows.

Eighteen witches hanged at Bury St. Edmunds on August 27th 1645. Papers were sold detailing their crimes and their convictions, explaining how Hopkins' searchers found proof of their guilt.

Similar methods were used to extract a confession from **Mary Lakeland** of Ipswich, probably the most famous of the Suffolk witches. A detailed account of this case can be found in John Glyde's *'A New Suffolk Garland'*

Known locally as **Mother Lakeland**, she had long been a dealer in potions and enchantments. She confessed to serving the devil for nearly 20 years. She said he furnished her with three imps, two little dogs and a mole, which she used to bewitch her husband who lay in great misery until his death. She also admitted to causing the death of Mr. Lawrence and his child simply because he had asked her to repay a debt of 12 shillings. She claimed in her confession that she had sent her mole to a maid of Mrs. Jennings to *'torment her and take away her life.'* Furthermore because Mr. Beale of Ipswich had refused to marry her granddaughter she had sent an imp to burn a new ship to which he had been appointed master, and caused a festering of his body, so half of it had rotted. What made this case special was the murder of a husband, which was classed as petty treason, and carried the penalty of being *'burned to ashes.'* It was said that on the day of her execution, a bunch of flesh in the shape of a dog grew upon the thigh of Mr. Beale and remained there until Mary Lakeland met her death, *'upon which it burst and began to heal.'*

Witches in this country were almost never burned to death. Yet, even after the repeal of the Witchcraft Act, criminal law demanded the burning of a wife who murdered her husband. **Mary Oliver** of Norwich suffered the same fate in 1658.

This savage remnant of medieval law was enacted as late as 1763 on Rushmere Heath. **Margery Beddingfield** and her lover **Richard Ringe** were both found guilty of the murder of John Beddingfield of Sternfield in Suffolk. Though Ringe hanged, the law still required that a murderous wife should be burned alive. However, it is likely that she was tied by the neck to the top of the stake, and a stool pulled away from under her feet, so she strangled to death before the faggots that were piled around her were set alight.

Increasingly, voices were raised in opposition to Matthew Hopkins and John Sterne. **John Gaule**, the vicar of Great Staughton near St. Neots asked, *"Who is this man who takes upon himself to be the giver of life or death? He could do no more harm if he were himself the servant of Satan. Hopkins' 'signs' mean that... every old woman, with a wrinkled face, a furry brow, a hairy lip, a gobber tooth, a squint eye, a squeaking voice or a scolding tongue... having a ragged coat on her back, a scull-cap on her head, a spindle in her hand, and a dog or cat by her side, is not only suspected, but pronounced for a witch."*

By the end of 1646, Hopkins was welcome nowhere and he ceased his witchfinding activities. What happened to him after that has long been a subject of speculation. It has been a popular belief that Hopkins himself was swum as a witch and found wanting. A contemporary poem *'Hudibras'* by Samuel Butler, appearing to describe Hopkins, gave support to this rumour as lines from the poem concluded:-

Who after prov'd himself a witch,
And made a rod for his own breech.

It is a lot more likely that, suffering from tuberculosis, Hopkins returned to Mistley near Manningtree where he died in August 1647.

Those who didn't hang

Eighteen witches hanged at Bury St. Edmund's on August 27th 1645. Though small numbers met their deaths at Ipswich and Aldeburgh, it is unclear just how many were convicted but eventually released. A commonly quoted statement is that hangings were delayed whilst pockets of Royalist resistance were put down, then a further fifty met their deaths. This seems slightly implausible. Matthew Hopkins had his greatest success operating autonomously, without the powers-that-be breathing down his neck. And anyway, he soon moved on to Norfolk and Cambridgeshire. The likeliest scenario is that a large number of those found guilty were imprisoned or pilloried, or both. Many being elderly, they may not have lived to return to their parishes. It may not even have been safe for them to go back to where the mania of the mob had seen them condemned.

It occurred to us that it would be valuable to search parish records to see how many of those listed for trial reappeared in their native parishes. Unfortunately, there is a large problem with this. It is well known amongst historians that parish records for the Civil War period are often missing. Churches were undergoing tremendous changes. Often registers and accounts books were hidden and no entries made for nine or ten years; sometimes if the books were lost, even longer periods remain unrecorded. Some parishes' records contain nothing surviving before about 1670, by which time most of our witches would have been dead anyway. However, using the information that is still available, it is possible to draw a few conclusions about the chances of survival of the Suffolk witches of 1645.

Most of the 18 that hanged in August that year came from Halesworth, Chattisham & Copdock. Their confessions appear to have been more damning and more acceptable to the court. By way of contrast, take the case of **Elizabeth Warne** of Framingham. Younger than many accused with her, she was watched and walked for three days and nights, confessing that *"pride and lustfulness had brought her to this and desired that she might be walked apace, for she had the devil in her."* Nevertheless, she was back in Framlingham, receiving poor relief a month later, and died as late as 1685. **Alexander Sussums** of Long Melford relied on the sympathy of the court. In his plea of guilty, he claimed his grandmother, mother and aunt had all been executed for witchcraft and he had been unable to resist the attentions of their imps, so causing the marks found by the searchers. He was discharged, and still living in 1648.

Matthew Hopkins picked upon the most vulnerable members of society. The parish records of Rattlesden make this clear. Four of the five indicted for witchcraft in 1645 (**Meribell Bedford, Henry Carre, Elizabeth Dickes, Old Mother Orvis** and **John Scarp**) had been in receipt of parish relief in 1643. Other information that is clear from the Rattlesden records is the large amount of intermarriage between the five families concerned. **Henry Carre** was described in the trial records as being a well-educated man. Despite Sterne finding the Devil's marks on him, he refused to confess to anything more than having two imps... *"like mice, hairy and heavy."* After several delays in bringing him to trial, he died in gaol. We believe one of the others, **Elizabeth Dickes**, may have hanged.

In the case of **Meribell Bedford**, there are several relevant entries in the overseers' accounts. In August 1645 there is a reference to *"Bedford being in prison 1s."* and *"to the jaylor at Bury 4s."* (September 1645) Ominously, an August 1646 reference mentions money being paid to Widow Miller for *"the* *care of the Bedford children."* Having said that, in 1650, there are mentions of *"Mel Bedford"* receiving various items of apparel. These might indicate she served a sentence that involved imprisonment and sessions in the pillory, as was common with those who did not hang. In her confession, she said… *"six yeares since, a black thing called Meribell asked her to deny God and Christ, promising that she should never want, but should be avenged of all her enemies."* Apparently the covenant had been sealed with blood from her little finger. She claimed to own four other imps including a spider called Joan and a wasp called Nann which sucked from her two or three times a week, and she… *"employed them to do much harm."* Oddly, over the next half-century, several people in the Rattlesden area named a daughter Mirabell.

Little is known of **Old Mother Orvis**, though members of her family and the Scarp family served as churchwardens for the parish around this time.

John Scarp appears to have died in 1646, having been married three times. He left a will. He was a sick man before his arrest and probably died in gaol. His surviving wife and children appear to have left the village of Rattlesden and may have found themselves more welcome in nearby Felsham, where other family members lived.

Seven men and women are known to have been *'found to be witches'* in Stowmarket by Matthew Hopkins. Of these only **Mary Fuller** almost certainly hanged (although someone of that name was buried at Stowmarket in 1680). Though a number of references suggest **Elizabeth Hobert** (or **Hubbard**) hanged, again a burial in 1682 of that name suggests otherwise. In her confession she claimed she had formed a covenant with the devil and caused her cousin harm so that he fell lame and continued in that way until he died. She confessed that her imps *"did suck twice or three times a week"* but had not been with her for a fortnight before her arrest.

Richard Foreman and **William Keeble** of Stowmarket were investigated by John Sterne under the orders of Matthew Hopkins, but found to be ignorant of all charges. Both men lived until 1666.

After The Witchfinder General

It might have been supposed that the discrediting of the Witchfinder General would have slowed the rate of witch trials, and briefly it did. However, whilst intellectuals may have had their doubts about such trials, the public were as fearful of witches and sorcerers as ever. A newly restored monarchy was not going to risk inciting public wrath to appease a few old local herbalists. So, the hangings continued.

Giles Fenderley was hanged in chains on Leaven Heath at Nayland in 1653, having confessed to murdering his wife after making a pact with the devil. He had served as a soldier in Flanders and had claimed he had secured protection so that he had taken a dozen bullets out of his clothes, but never suffered any harm. His dubious defence was that the devil had claimed the life of his wife, so he had killed her.

Two Lowestoft girls found themselves indicted in 1664 for bewitching a number of their neighbours. **Rose Cullender** and **Amy Duny** were the targets of a host of accusations. Dorothy Durent described how her child, becoming sick with fits and a strange distemper, sought advice from **Dr. Jacob**, a wise man from Yarmouth, who advised hanging up the child's blanket in the chimney corner all day. At night, he said, should she find anything in the blanket, she was to throw it on the fire. Following his instructions, a large toad was found, which flashed and crackled in the fire with a great deal of noise. Amy Duny was later seen, much scorched and burnt about the face. Later, Dorothy Durent was made lame, and continued on crutches until the end of the trial, when she made a remarkable recovery.

A

TRYAL

OF

WITCHES,

AT THE

ASSIZES

HELD AT

Bury St. Edmonds for the County of *SUFFOLK*; on the Tenth day of *March*, 1664.

BEFORE

Sir MATTHEW HALE Kt.

THEN

Lord Chief Baron of His Majesties Court of EXCHEQUER.

Taken by a Perſon then Attending the Court

LONDON,

Printed for *William Shrewsbery* at the Bible in *Duck-Lane.* 1682.

Other accusations included those from children who had become deprived of speech, and had vomited up pins and nails, which were produced in the court as 'evidence'.

The prosecution was given greater credibility by the appearance of the highly respected **Dr. Browne** of Norwich, who was convinced these children had been bewitched. After that, the testimonies came thick and fast. It was said John Soham and Robert Sherringham, whose carts had touched and slightly damaged Rose Cullender's house, had suffered a catalogue of misfortunes - livestock dying, clothes infested with lice and gateways that mysteriously narrowed so as not to allow carts through.

Ann Sandeswel testified to her geese having been destroyed, and her chimney being blighted, causing it to fall. Also she told a tale of a firkin of fish sent by boat to her from her brother, that reports said had refused to stay on board and had literally *"gone to the devil."*

Lord Justice Hale took the unusual decision not to summarise the evidence for the jury. He did however emphasize his belief in the existence of witches and the reliability of traditional forms of evidence. The two girls were found guilty and executed on March 17th 1664. They never made a confession. In later years, **Arthur Onslow**, speaker of the House of Commons, reported that Judge Hale was greatly altered in his opinions regarding witches, and showed much concern for what had befallen Amy Duny and Rose Cullender.

Sir John Holt, presiding over the Suffolk Lent Sessions in 1694 was more circumspect. He was not to know, but England had already hanged its last witches. **Temperance Lloyd**, **Susannah Edwards** and **Mary Trembles** of Bideford in Devon were hanged in 1682. **Alice Molland** was sentenced to death at Exeter in 1684, but in spite of many references to the contrary, probably died the following year, no execution having taken place.

Widow Chambers of Upaston (Ubbeston) was arrested in 1693 and committed to Beccles Gaol where she was walked until she confessed that she had caused the death by witchcraft of her husband and Lady Blois (although that lady's relatives said she died a fair death). Before Widow Chambers could be brought to trial, she died.

In the spring of 1694, **Justice Holt** heard a number of indictments against **Phillipa Munnings** of Hartest. Some of the counts dated back ten years. It was said she had threatened her landlord, Thomas Pannell: *"Thy nose shall lie upward in the churchyard before Sunday next."* This was an unfortunate prediction, which turned out to be true. One witness in court claimed to have seen her take two imps from a basket, one white, one black; and others swore she possessed an evil spirit in the shape of a polecat.

The accusations included three 'bewitching to death's, including that of James Parkin, whose body was never found. She was acquitted of all charges, and protested her innocence until her death two years later.

That same year, the same Judge saw **Margaret Elnore** acquitted on the dubious evidence of having witch marks on her body. She had been accused of sending lice and sickness. Her grandmother and aunt had been hanged as witches and a midwife who examined her claimed she had witch marks on her body *"plainer than theirs had been."*

What is clear from these and other similar cases is that Sir John Holt's scepticism contributed greatly in bringing an end to the gross injustices of the witchcraft trials.

Suffolk owed him a lot, and it was to Suffolk he retired, having turned down the post of Lord Chancellor to King William III. He was buried in Redgrave Church, where a grand monument describes him as... *'the watchful upholder, the keen defender, the brave guardian of liberty and the law of England.'*

The last witchcraft conviction in England happened in 1712. In spite of the Judge's direction, the jury found **Jane Wenham** of Walkern, near Stevenage guilty, and Mr. Justice Powell was

forced to pass a sentence of death. The feeble evidence offered revolved around the howling and scratching of her cats which were reputed to howl like children and stare at passers by from the windows of her house. The enlightened judge delayed the hanging long enough to obtain a Royal pardon for **Jane Wenham** (pictured here). For the rest of her life, she had to be hidden from the mobs that had vowed to see justice done as the jury had intended. It wasn't until 1736 that the Witchcraft Act (1604) of James I was repealed, and even then, the decision was none too popular.

You can change the law, but you can't change people's opinions and beliefs so easily. As the first story in this book shows, superstition held good in Suffolk for at least another two centuries. By the early eighteenth century, we had local newspapers being published, copies of most of which survive to this day. It is to these we are able to turn to show how attitudes changed little in Suffolk, in spite of what was passed as law at Westminster.

There are several reports appearing in our book, *'Grave Reports'* which show how the practice of burying people who had committed suicide at the nearest crossroads, with a stake driven through their heart persisted a long time in Suffolk. So too did other superstitious practices including occasional instances of mob justice against those unfortunate enough to be suspected of witchcraft.

The following lines are a facsimile of those appearing on a loose paper at the end of the parish register of Monks Eleigh.

> Decr the 19th 1748. Alice the wife of Thos Green, labourer, was swam, malicious & wicked people having raised an ill report of her, for being a Witch.

In an article in the Suffolk Sage Vol. 5 (Oct. 1993), Sheila Hardy relates the story of **Grace Pett**, who died in 1744. A farmer's wife living just outside Ipswich consulted a 'wise man' about an outbreak of sheep disease on their farm, and was advised to burn one sheep to rid the flock of the curse afflicting them. However the flames did not burn the animal's feet. That night, Grace Pett, who was widely regarded as being responsible for the sheep disease, burned to death as she slept, leaving nothing but her feet and hands. The room showed no evidence of the fire.

> By a letter from Woodbridge in Suffolk, we learn that the country people about Aspal Stonham in that neighbourhood are still so full of ignorance and superstition that they imagine there are several witches and wizards in that neighbourhood and they have tied up two or three old people in sheets with cords round their middles and flung them into the rivers to see if they could save themselves. But whether the cords held them up or Providence supported them, the poor wretches, it is certain have got safe to shore. This has confirmed their opinion and to them they attribute their loss of cattle, bad harvests &c, and insist that these poor wretches shall be tried by the church bible whether they are witches or no, for if witches, the bible will turn round and not weigh them down or such idle stuff.
>
> Norwich Gazette: Sept. 1752

The Gentleman's Magazine contained a number of stories and comments that demonstrated it was not only the uneducated who still believed in witches in the eighteenth century. One writer signing himself G. M. suggested in a letter of 1753 that as a result of the repeal of the witch act, *'The devil may be truly said to be let loose among us.'* An article in the same magazine in February 1759 described how one **Susanna Hannokes**, an elderly woman had been accused by a neighbour for bewitching her spinning wheel so it would not go round. Depositions having been put before the magistrate, she was taken to the church, stripped of her clothes and weighed against the bible, *"which to the no small mortification of her accuser she outweighed, and was honourably acquitted of the charge."*

In a more dramatic example of mob rule, an elderly couple by the name of **Osborne** in Hertfordshire in 1751 were stripped naked, tied thumbs to toes, dragged two miles and ducked in a muddy stream. **Ruth Osborne** died as a result of this treatment and **Thomas Colley**, the ringleader, was hanged in chains for her murder. Reputedly many thousands stood at a distance, refusing to be spectators of his death and muttering that it was *"...a hard case to hang a man for destroying an old wicked woman that had done so much mischief by her witchcraft."*

A much earlier image of the swimming of a witch, but little had really changed since 1612 when this picture was first published

More locally, towards the end of the eighteenth century, an old lady of Stanningfield, appealed to her local magistrates, to protect her against accusations of witchcraft, as this article from the Bury & Norwich Post for June 20th 1792 shows.

> In the courſe of an examination relative to a pauper on Wedneſday ſe'nnight before Sir Charles Davers, Bart. and the Rev. John Ord, at the Angel Inn, in this town, an old woman, belonging to the pariſh of Staningfield, mentioned that another had called her a Witch, which ſhe ſaid had very much diſordered her in her head, but the juſtices told her they could take no cognizance thereof. On Wedneſday laſt, however, it appeared before the ſame magiſtrates, that, in conſequence of this allegation, the woman had voluntarily ſubmitted to the uſual ordeal;—at firſt it was propoſed to weigh her againſt the church-bible, but the clergyman refuſed to lend the ſame, when her huſband, brother, and another man, tied a rope round her body, and caſt her into a horſe-pond, from whence, as ſhe was found to ſink, they dragged her out, almoſt lifeleſs. On the men being rebuked for this egregious inſtance of folly, in complying with ſo extraordinary a requeſt, and particularly the huſband, he ſaid that he thought it better to indulge her therein, than to ſuffer her to deſtroy herſelf, which he was certain ſhe would have done, had ſhe not undergone this trial.

This story turns up in a number of places. Other references add details not recorded in the paper. Her name was **Mrs. Greygoose** and her six cats named Silcock, Wisky, Turntail, Toby, Tarran and Tegg were regarded as her 'imps.' The spot chosen was Hoggage (or Hoggarts) Green, in a pond near the churchyard. (This detail comes from the proceedings of Suffolk Inst. of Archaeology Vol. III, which incorrectly dates it as having happened in 1795) She sank, proving her innocence, but as we can see, she was dragged out *'almost lifeless.'*

Another better-documented case was reported both locally and nationally in July 1825, when a sixty-seven year old man was swum for a wizard at Wickham Skeith in the presence of hundreds of people.

> **Isaac Stebbings**…earns a living as a huckster; and hard by his cottage lives a thatcher whose wife unfortunately is afflicted in mind. In that same parish, there happens to be a farmer

The 'Grimmer' at Wickham Skeith

whose mind is also occasionally disturbed. As in former days of gross credulity and ignorance, some one or other put forth the surmise that these two afflicted persons are bewitched, and Stebbings was spoken of as the worker of the mischief ...Besides this, the village shoemaker persisted that one morning as Stebbings passed two or three times before his house, he could not "make" his wax - the ingredients would neither melt nor mix. Dubbed a wizard beyond all doubt, poor Stebbings, ignorant as his neighbours, and teased beyond bearing, proposed at length, of himself, the good old fashioned ordeal of "sink or swim."

Saturday at two o'clock in a large pond called the Grimmer, on Wickham Green, four men were appointed to walk into the water with him, and the constable of the parish engaged to attend and keep the peace. The sides of the pond were crowded with spectators - men, women and children.

The article describes how, clearly unsure how to proceed, the trialists attempted without success, to get Stebbings to sink. They sat on various parts of his body in a vain attempt to sink him. These trials kept the poor old fellow three quarters of an hour in the pond, and he came out *'more dead than alive.'*

Still some were not satisfied. Another man, they said, of his age and size, ought to be *'swam with him'* ...and a man named **Tom Wilding** of Bacton parish nearby was named for his companion. The story now got more wind, and hundreds of people from all the neighbouring parishes attended to witness the second ordeal.

> It is now gravely told that the afflicted farmer alluded to above, was unusually perturbed: he cried out, "I can see the imps all about me; I must frighten them away with my voice."
>
> To complete the affair, a respectable farmer in a neighbouring parish has been, it is said, to some 'cunning man', and learnt, to a certainty that Stebbings is a wizard. The sum of £3 was paid for this intelligence upon the assurance that Stebbings should be "killed by inches." Of course, it was not the cunning man who parted with the money.

The newspaper account describes how the rector of the parish and his churchwardens intervened, to the disappointment of the crowd, but doubtless the relief, of Isaac Stebbings. It concludes...

> Even now in the nineteenth century, a portion of the populace - perhaps a considerable portion - retaining the foolish prejudices of their forefathers, believe that there are witches and wizards still.
>
> Suffolk Chronicle: July 16th 1825

It may comfort some to know that Isaac Stebbings lived another twenty-two years, dying at the ripe old age of 88.

In our books 'Newspapers in Suffolk:' Volumes III & IV, we refer to several local witchcraft stories. These two are worthy of further mention.

> **WITCHCRAFT IN ELY** - There is an old woman, at Ely, named **Ann Gotobed** who is supposed to possess the power of witchcraft. ...Her landlord, one Samuel Bartingale, a worthy

old carpenter, not liking to reside near so evil a genius, ejected her and the consequence was poor Sam was taken ill. The cause was evident; he was bewitched, and the neighbours met in the sick man's chamber and solemnly deliberated upon the matter, when upon the suggestion of an old lady of seventy, it was agreed that a horse shoe should be nailed over the door.

Bury Post: March 18th 1846

The article goes on to explain that this well-known cure for witchcraft failed at first, but when they looked closer, they realised they had nailed up an ass's shoe. Once the mistake had been corrected, the sick man recovered.

WITCHCRAFT IN 1855

In the parish of Norton, there lives a famous old woman of the name of **Osborn** - and she is said to have the powers of a witch. The powers she possesses are of hereditary origin - her mother, old **Mrs. Talbot** of Cotton, having been notorious for her fortune-telling and witchery. "She told my fortune very accurately," said my informant. "I was to have a man who should use a very heavy hammer - knock knock knock - and I was to have always plenty of bread and meat in the tub. And true it was - I married a blacksmith - and have never wanted for anything yet. One day the old woman called at my house - but not having time just then to talk to her, or give her anything - she went away a little dissatisfied: next day, a pig we had in the sty was taken in a very strange way - it moaned about - it grunted - poked its head over the top of the sty - refused to eat - and was altogether in such a way as we never saw a pig before. "What can be the matter," said my husband? "Oh," said I, "I know;" so I ran for a knife, slipped a piece off the tail of the pig - and threw it into the fire - and the pig got well directly.

This bizarre collection of tales continued, with mention of the power of 'witch bottles' as a protection from the likes of Mrs. Osborn.

In the parish of Ashfield, a poor woman is in a deranged state, and she declares that old Mrs Osborn has done it; she is in the greatest terror every time a little wind rumbles in her stomach and says it is the old woman inside of her, and to get out of her way, she is tempted to destroy herself. Her fiends have tried to dissolve the spell. They have pared the poor woman's nails very close, but they failed twice in the experiment. Unfortunately the cork flew out of the bottle every time. The bottle should burst, but they mean to try it again, and they hope with a better result.

Mrs Osborn wished a young man at Elmswell to marry her daughter; but finding that he was paying attention to some other girl, the old woman resolved to have her revenge; so one day as the young man was sitting in his cottage, a strange cat came in and flew at him: it struck him directly that it was one of the old woman's imps, so he catches the cat and places her feet in the fire. Now this did not burn the cat's feet, but it did the old woman's, and she has been laid by with burnt feet ever since.

Bury Post: August 8th 1855

It is clear from the tone of the article that the correspondent regards such stories as worthy only of his contempt and he concludes…

I think enough has been stated to shew the profound ignorance and amazing credulity still existing amongst a certain class of the community; and if these remarks should have the effect of dispelling some of the darkness which prevails in their minds, by holding up to ridicule the excessive absurdity of fortune-telling and witchcraft, at the same time that they may afford some amusement to your more intelligent readers, I shall consider my object to be accomplished.

It is interesting to note there are still people living in Norton today who can remember being told tales of "**Witchy Osborn**" whose broomstick could be heard periodically going 'click, click, click!' each time it touched down as the witch flew low along the road.

Quacks, mystics and fortune-tellers have regularly featured in our local newspapers, though it is clear from the tone of such reports that the reporters were anxious to make it clear that they were not fooled, even if the rest of East Anglia was.

John Kiniman, a poor shoemaker of Nisby was, by upwards of a thousand spectators (very near relations to the wise men of Gotham) from all the neighbouring villages, conducted to a great pond in Kelmarsh Lordship, and underwent the discipline of the ducking stool, for being suspected as a wizard, and conspiring with the Devil, his master, to prevent the lazy dairy women's making good butter and cheese etc. There was also one Barwick, who, in his great integrity to see justice done, offered himself to (and did) take the same diversion, in order to prove that the wizard could not be plunged under water so soon and easy as himself, tho' it is said, that another dipping would have brought many of the undertakers of this political way of trying wizards and witches to have made but an indifferent figure at our ensuing Assizes, as was the fate of some of their neighbouring country folks a few years since, when a poor old woman lost her life.

Ipswich Gazette: July 5th 1735

FORTUNE TELLING The wife of a labourer named **Stephen Hatch**, residing at Little Bromley was robbed of £8 10s., on Thursday last, by a gipsy who induced the credulous woman to allow her to deposit the treasure in a small box, under pretence of giving her victim a peep into the future.

West Suffolk and North Essex Free Press: May 15th 1856

LAVENHAM - A most singular annoyance commenced at **Mrs. East**'s of the Blackbird Public House in this town, which has continued, at intervals up to this day. Scarcely a whole pane is left in any of the windows at the back of the house and very few have escaped in front... Many a grandmother's marvellous tale has been adduced to prove that this has been occasioned by WITCHES AND WIZARDS. It has to be hoped that the activity of the officers, and the reward which is offered, will in a short time bring the "hobgoblins" to the seat of justice.

Suffolk Chronicle: May 17th 1823

Witches and their charms continued to be part of the folklore of Suffolk, as this Breckland story of 1856 shows.

> On Monday night, between 10 and 11 a.m., a man was going up to the house of Mrs. Flower of Feltwell place when he saw some men in the yard. He immediately informed **Johnathan Flower**, a powerful young man, who armed himself with a hunting stick and... proceeded into the yard. When opening the door of the barn, three men made their escape in different directions. Two got away, but the other got over one gate and tried to get over a second, when Mr. Flower aimed a blow which felled him, the hook catching him on the side of the head. He proved to be **Tom Gathercole**, who for many years has defied the blue-coated men, although suspected of being concerned in many robberies. He was removed to the Oak Inn at Feltwell, where his wounds were dressed by Mr. Archer, the surgeon. ...Many congratulations have been received by Mr. Flower for having at last secured one who for many years was a great dread to farmers, for it is said his mother was a witch, and at her decease willed her son a little talisman which would at any time save him from the hands of justice. (Bury & Norwich Post)

There were those who made it their mission to protect the old, the disabled and the downright odd from accusations of dabbling in witchcraft. One such was **Richard Grey**. Born in Bury around 1770, of a wealthy family, Grey studied law as a young man but on inheriting a fortune at the age of 22, he spent the rest of his life attempting to educate ignorant credulous rural folk and convince them their more eccentric neighbours were not responsible for every misfortune that came their way. Especially along the Suffolk coast a lasting faith in witchcraft was still strong in 1800, sometimes leading to great cruelty. On many occasions, Richard Grey found himself at odds with the local community when he tried to make them see sense and release their victims before any real harm could be done. There are tales told of his attendance at Potters Bridge near Southwold, which was reputed to be a favourite place for swimming witches.

On one occasion, when trying to reason with an angry mob in Orford, Grey was tied to a stake with brushwood placed around him. It seemed he would be burned alive for sympathising with witches, thus making him one too in the eyes of the superstitious rabble. Luckily, he was permitted to escape. Gradually he became known along the coast around Aldeburgh where he lived, and people became more prepared to accept there was no such thing as witchcraft. Richard Grey died in a boating accident on the Alde on new year's day, 1851. His body was never recovered.

The famous Hedingham witchcraft case of 1864 demonstrated that the lynch mob was still capable of dispensing 'justice' well over a century after we stopped trying witches.

Emma Smith, the wife of a beerhouse keeper of Ridgewell and **Samuel Stammers**, a carpenter of Sible Hedingham were charged with causing the death of an old man named **Dummy**. Dummy, as his nickname suggests, was deaf and dumb. He lived in a hovel near Sible Hedingham and was about 80 years of age. His odd gestures and excitable behaviour led a number of locals to believe he was possessed. He travelled the villages of Northern Essex telling fortunes and selling love-spells. Three or four small dogs followed him everywhere he went.

On one of his trips to Ridgewell, Emma Smith refused him permission to lodge at her husband's inn. He showed his displeasure by stroking his stick and using threatening gestures. Soon after, Emma Smith became ill and was convinced she had been bewitched by Dummy. Though she pleaded with him to remove the curse and even offered him three sovereigns to stay at her house, he refused to do so. On the 3rd August 1863, when he was drinking at the Swan public house in Sible Hedingham, a crowd gathered in support of Emma Smith. Dummy was roughly handled, his clothes torn; he was struck with a stick and dragged down to a nearby stream. The court report in the Bury Post stated that Mrs. Smith had shouted, "You old devil, you served me out, now I will serve you out."

Then she and Stammers shoved him into the stream, and as fast as he tried to climb out, they pushed him back. Eventually finding himself in some depth of water, he began to struggle for his life and one of the villages was reported as calling out, "If someone does not take that old man out he will die in a minute." Though Stammers did haul him out, Dummy lay for some time in an exhausted state until they took him home and left him in his wet clothes all night. Twenty-four hours later he was dead. The post mortem showed that he died from disease of the kidneys produced by immersion in water and sleeping in wet clothes. Having heard the judge's summing up, the jury found the prisoners guilty and they were sentenced to six months' hard labour.

The following letter appeared in the East Anglian Miscellany in 1904.

> In Stowmarket, we have a woman who is said to have inherited the gift from her mother, who cuts for the spleen, an imaginary affection, the symptoms of which are probably attributable to indigestion or anaemia. Anyhow the process of the cure is as follows...
>
> The woman cuts the back of the ear slightly with a razor, dips her finger into the exuding blood, marks the forehead with the sign of a cross, mutters an incantation, puts a plaster of the expressed oil of mace upon the pit of the stomach, orders them to chew rhubarb root before each meal, and the spleen will be cured. She charges a fee of 5s, an important factor in the treatment.
>
> Esculapius, Stowmarket.

And still such beliefs held good. Local Newspapers in September 1904 published the following case from Bottisham near Cambridge.

> Last year, a wood merchant aged only 27 was imprisoned for cruelty to his three horses. He thought they had been bewitched by an enemy, and to remove the spell he gave them a broth which he made by boiling some nails, a penny worth of pins and pieces of a horse's hoof over a fire with incantations. It is by no means improbable that this native of 'civilised' England has occasionally dipped his coin into the missionary's bag to help convert 'the heathen in his darkness.'

The Daily Mail in February 1919 reported the case of a Swaffham farmer who, believing he had a cow bewitched, put a red-hot poker into the churn and *'the spirit went up in a flame which lighted up the dairy.'*

Though we can read these accounts with a mixture of horror and amusement, stories still appear from time to time that show belief in the forces of the occult is alive and well across most parts of rural Britain. References to witches crop up in the most unlikely places. In reply to a letter from a lady trying unsuccessfully to lose weight, the Psychic Correspondent of CHAT magazine in 2003 began:

> *I sense that for the past seven years, your life has been one of trials and tribulations. Looking at my witchdoctor bones, I see that after a trip to Austria, you'll find the strength to stick to a healthy eating plan.*

They do say that the ghost of Matthew Hopkins still haunts the area around Old Mistley, near Manningtree. Now what would he make of that?